A Bold Walk to Happiness

Brett Miller

A Bold Walk to Happiness
Copyright © 2022 by Brett Miller

Tellwell Talent
www.tellwell.ca

ISBN
978-0-2288-8142-1 (Hardcover)
978-0-2288-8141-4 (Paperback)
978-0-2288-8143-8 (eBook)

What makes you happy in the grand picture of things is a pretty broad question, if you ask me. The thing we have to look at is what will make us happy. I tell you happiness is not going to be in something or even people per say but rather in being truly happy with yourself to go out there in the universe and kick ass. Also, you can show your love to others because you have a love for yourself within.

Let me tell you a story. When I was twenty-five years old, I was going home from my parents' house, driving my car, and I was getting severe chest pains. The more I drove, the worse it got. I walked into my house, where some renters lived with me. Also, my sister lived with me. When I walked in the door, the pain worsened. I went upstairs, returned ten minutes later, and collapsed on the living room floor. I immediately got dizzy and had severe pain because I couldn't breathe. My sister came down the stairs and called 911. The ambulance showed up, and when I made it to the hospital, I couldn't comprehend how I got there. Nurses came in and hooked me up too many things, and then in walked my buddy's ex-girlfriend. I'm like, *Here we go, the nurse who likes to steal napkins from the Dairy Queen; what a class act.* At this time, she stabbed some needles in me, laughing the whole time. I also had an IV bag hooked up. The pain kept getting worse, and by now I was passed out. When I woke up, the lights were out.

The doctor came in, and he said, "Good morning, Mr. Miller. The good news is you're not dead. The bad news is you have a blood clot that started in your right leg that was fourteen inches long. Half of it broke off into both of your lungs, and the other half went into your heart. You just had a stroke, and I'm not sure how you're still sitting here breathing. We will try our best to keep you going, but I can't guarantee."

My priest came in to pray for me as the days went by. I remember we were talking about the love of Jesus and how we can conquer all by what he put in us. At that moment, I knew Jesus. Still, I didn't know God at this type of hour. Having a doctor tell you "I'm glad you're not dead" was an absolute miracle in my eyes and made me realize how life is pretty short. I asked myself what I wanted to do with my life because what I was currently doing was not fulfilling. *Am I going to keep on doing the same old stuff, or am I going to explore my options and set out to find what I want to do with my life?* Let me ask you this: When you go to sleep at night, are you fulfilled? And hey! You may make great money, but are you happy to the core? When we look at true happiness, we have to be satisfied with ourselves, but if you're doing something right now that you hate or just like, how will that work for you long term? We live in this "kind-of-like" society. *I like this person, but I don't get fired up to be with them. I like this job, but I don't go jumping out of bed to go after it and light it up. I want to get married someday to this person, but I won't be upset if it does not happen. I like this business adventure, but I will not get too frustrated if it doesn't work out.* When we look at our goal, dream, gift, and what we were born to do, we can't have a Plan B because Plan B is a waste of time. It would be best to only have a Plan A. *I will do this come hell or high water; this is what God has put inside me to do. I will get the job done no matter what, and no one will separate God and me for what he has planned for my life.* It's hard for me not to laugh when I see people always running to people to give them an answer. Let me ask you this about me, someone with sin and flaws. How do you expect me to provide you with something that God can give you? I hate to tell you it will never happen.

What amazed me was how little I knew and how weak my vocabulary was when I first started reading the Bible. When we think of things that can create unhappiness, some examples come to mind. Social media will plant this seed inside of you; if you spend too much time with it, you will become obsessed with comparing your life to someone else's. You will be looking at their stuff and going, *Wow, my life doesn't look as good as theirs. How can I expect these thoughts of happiness long term when I'm constantly comparing my life to someone else's?* Understand that your life is unique to you and that God gave us all a unique life at birth.

Another thing that comes to mind is lust and pornography. Pornography will give you this sense to only look at a person's physical appearance and body and what it could do for you. By basing the relationship on sex, when we look at someone lustfully, rather than getting to know the person, we may find out that this person who has the desirable physical appearance does not have the attitude or personality we were looking for. Here are some helpful tips for modern ladies: if you want a committed relationship with a man, start by getting to know the man before having sex with him. See if he has willpower and see if he likes you as a person and not just based on what you can do for him sexually. Understand this, though: unless the man likes dudes or is very deep-rooted in his religion and committed to celibacy before marriage, he will never say no. If you remove all your clothes for a man and expect him to have the willpower to say no, guess what? It will never happen. He's not going to say, "Oh, don't worry about it. I will catch you next time." Men, in general, aren't programmed like this. Also, a man can have sex with a woman and feel absolutely nothing after. Just because he has sex with you doesn't mean he will want a relationship after the fact. If I see a woman willing to let it all loose for next to nothing, I don't look at her as relationship material. It's like this: *You're showing me you don't respect yourself enough to let me fight for you, so how do I expect you to show me any respect in a relationship? And how do I expect you to say you could love me when you're willing to give it up for next to nothing?*

There is a difference between having sex and making love. Sex will always be driven by having this "kind of" attitude at the back of your mind: *Let's try this relationship out. If it does not work, no sweat; I'm not going to be to upset.* Making love with a person is different; you feel a deep-rooted connection with this person, and you give a shit about the outcome, and you will be upset and hurt if things don't work out. I'm looking for a woman who likes who she is, who is a bit of a rebel, and who isn't always going to tell me good news. Why, you might ask? Because I want a challenge. I get bored very quickly. For the most part, I would say that men don't care what a woman does for a living or how much money she makes. We are happy to date a girl who works at the corner store. In the grand picture of things, what a woman does for a living is not a priority. Men don't care about labels, but if you are a career woman, understand you are making a sacrifice if you decide to do so. Hey, there's nothing wrong with that.

Here's a funny story: I remember back when I was going to high school, I was very intrigued with this one woman, and from a physical standpoint, she was not a girl you would go, "Oh wow, she is a knockout. Her physical beauty is radiating." No, not at all, but what I found about her when we all hung out in a group was her level of intelligence. She was super intuitive and knew what she wanted and where she was going. Her ability to convey and project with absolute certainty that she knew what she was doing and had her goals written down and how she wanted to accomplish them I found to be a huge turn on. For myself, over the years, as I have grown as a person and advanced to a new level and new heights, I have always tried to hang around more intelligent people than me because I realize if I keep doing this, the more my thinking is going to expand and the more of an impact I'm going to make not only on my life but also on the lives of others.

Recently, over the last few years, I have become good friends with a priest. I started going to a different church because I moved, and at the end of the day, I'm glad I did. He has become a mentor to me and is a book of knowledge when I talk to him. It's hard to fathom, but I was raised Catholic and brought up in the church, and until I started going to his church, I had not experienced the gospel quite like that since I was a bean sprout, growing up in Ontario, Canada. It's not really a common thing when you're a thirty-year-old man to say to someone, "Yah, I go to church every Sunday." Church is almost like a foreign thing to most people. For myself, if I were to give my two cents, Millennials and Gen Z, for the majority, are constantly into so many different things. The number of other things I've heard people are into is astronomical. It's an endless supply. For myself, when I go to church, I am very engaged and get a lot out of the sermon not only because I am very into it, but also because of the amount of energy and confidence my priest exudes when he is up in the pulpit. Like anything in life, people follow strength. Strength usually comes with a certain amount of authority, like when Jesus got mad the one time and turned the table of the money changers (the people who were committing wrongful acts). When I get up to speak in the pulpit as a lector, or when I am speaking anywhere else, I speak with authority. Why? Because people listen more closely to what you're saying when there is depth and character in your voice and you're not there to mess around and keep it boring. Ask yourself this: How long would you say your attention span is, for the most part? Would you say you are someone who can listen for hours on end about something, or would you say your attention almost comes in spurts, to a certain degree? By being engaged in anything, there is going to have to be a level of wanting to know more. There needs to be a bit of mystery. The way you articulate and project your speech will determine how you are perceived and how people react to you. I'm going to tell you this: Not everyone will be on board and believe what you're saying, and that's ok, because not everyone will be for you. If I had a dollar for every time I thought someone would be supportive, I would be a multimillionaire by now, but believing in yourself to an unstoppable degree requires looking at something besides yourself and in the form of a higher power. In my opinion, the gospel is the most motivational book ever written. There are so many underlying stories that can relate to something going on with your own life right here and right now.

I found when I first started reading the Bible how poor and how intrinsic, rationalized, and common my grammar was. For the vast majority of people I encounter, what I was projecting in my speech wasn't too methodical; it was just something that was stagnant. You could say I was not getting to the ulterior motive. I was just basically saying stuff for the gratification of pleasing people, and over time, that is never a good thing. Don't be afraid of ruffling some feathers and standing up when it is necessary to do. I'm at the point in my life where I seek to do what's right, and if it means breaking some rules, then so be it. I would rather do the right thing and ask for forgiveness later than do the wrong thing and keep living not in the truth in a life that doesn't align with my beliefs.

When you first step out and decide to bet on yourself, and always had the right stuff, it will be scary. I've always been an underdog type of person. I never had anyone ever tell me "You're so exceptional." Things I love to do have always been work for me. Funny story: I remember when I was going to elementary school, Our Lady of Fatima it was called, and they dragged me into a room the one day. This was about Grade Three. They were like, "Well, Mr. Miller, since you don't learn like the rest of the students, we are going to put you on this individual education plan." This was another way of secretly telling me that I was stupid. I saw that on my report card all the way up till I graduated high school. It caused me great anger and frustration. I felt like, *You don't know me for shit, and how dare you try to give your opinion of me, because guess what? It's not going to become my reality. I deserve better than that.* I believe the education system has failed a lot of people. In life and with how things are structured, there are no guarantees. I know dozens of people who are way more educated than me, yet at the end of the day, they have no better job than me. How does that make sense at the end of the day if you always rely on people to give you this amazing answer to the extent that "If you do this, you will have it all figured out"? Life doesn't work like that. It is full of ups and downs with wins and losses, and the losses will usually far exceed the wins.

The thing about happiness is that it's all about progress. If we are all each and every day progressing to achieve one of our goals, then negative notions usually take the back seat. Learn to be mission-driven. *What will this mean if I do this?* and also *What will this mean in the lives of others if I fully dive into what I have been called to do?* Because it's about the calling. You can feel something in your heart if it directly aligns with who you are and your being of existence. There is no force on this entire Earth that will stop it if you are fully committed. Recognize who is for you and who is against you. I have done so many nice things for people who could not care at the end of the day what I do or who I am. It's fascinating how the human brain works, especially at this point in time. It's fascinating how far we have come as a society. A lot of things have become superficial and are based on looking for a glandular reward or a feeling from something or a mindset of *I'm deserving*. It's like the world does not owe me anything: I am the author and finisher of my story. Life is what you make it, who you choose to surround yourself with, and the energy you attract into your life. Doing what's right can be peaceful but also scary at the same time because you never know what the outcome will be until it happens. Let me ask you this: Does God want you to do what's right or wrong? Telling the truth and being real will get you to new heights and greater expansion, and hey, it might cost you something. Still, you will know. You will not be pondering a question, wondering "What if?" Life is way too short to ask "What if?" If you get shunned in the process, then so be it. Understand that not everyone will like you and like what you have to offer. People frown on stuff they don't have. I'm at a point where I am mission-driven. What do I want to accomplish? How will I do it? What is this gift God has put inside of me to fulfill? I GET LOST when I get writing and when I do other things like public speaking. When I'm in the zone, you could say I literally could go for hours as I write and write; I look at this book as a study guide. Read it and apply some steps you can take to your own life. I look at this book as a tool because multiple people have coached me and coaching costs. Coaching is not a cheap hobby, so how do I take some great ideas that I have learned in my own life to apply them to a book someone can afford and be able to keep with them? That's a win. Not only can I give back, but I can share a piece of me. I have taken the time and energy to write from the heart.

As we go through life, various things will bring us down. But how do we react to our emotions in the current moment? Do we focus on the good or the bad? Everything that goes up must come down in the rollercoaster of life. Ask yourself this personal question: When you wake up till the time you go to bed, on average, how many different emotions would you say you experience daily? I'm sure it's more than one. Ask yourself what you are allowing yourself to tolerate daily. Is your brain progressing into joyful harmonious thoughts, or is it keeping you stagnant and frustrated? When I think about emotions flowing freely, I think about my surroundings and the energy I let surround me. This can be compared to hanging around someone who mistreats you and won't go out of their way to do anything. In contrast, someone kind to you would give you the shirt off their back and exchange meaningful conversation. Which one do you think could lead to long-term results? The choice is pretty obvious. This would be like me going, "Well, I'm not too fond of the response I'm getting to what I'm writing, so I'm going to give up and try something else." Without commitment, nothing significant ever happens. I could quit and try something else, but guess what? The problem is still there when I leave, and it follows me. Without changing my mind first, the same old habits and patterns will follow me wherever I go. The old saying goes, "You can buy a new car, but if you put the old man in the new car, you'll still have the old experience." A life led by love is the recipe for a win or a future win. When we weren't given something when we were young, it's sometimes hard to justify when it happens years down the road. We think, *This is too good to be true; something is bound to mess up*, but I guess we are all human. Something is bound to happen. We all make mistakes, and we all mess up from time to time. Embrace it, and don't be so hard on yourself all the time. I have always battled this over the years because I'm very hard on myself to reach my goals. After all, it's all up to me, no one else. This book isn't going to write itself. I take responsibility that it's on me and only me. If I don't get what I want out of this book and express myself in a way that is readable and presentable, then that's totally on me.

Understand the need to take action and then some more action. Set up the right pieces to win, because guess what? Even though it's your responsibility to make it happen, you must also understand that you can't do it all alone. Surround yourself with people you can learn from, and work with people who are better at something than you. If I want good insights from the Bible, I go to my priest and he can break down exactly what it means to the very last word because he has mastered his calling. At the end of the day, he is a man of God. I could tell you stories that I know from the Bible, but when he tells it, it's on a whole other level, and by the time he is done his sermon, I always get something out of it. I usually go, "Jeez, I never thought about it like that." Because once you have mastered something, there are no limits to what you can accomplish. The possibilities are endless and unstoppable, because when you're in that type of zone where you are the author and the finisher by what you do and know the absolute ins and outs, it will affect everything in your life in a positive way. You are reaching and stretching to something newer and greater, something out of this world. When people look at you, they will say, "Jeez, that person made that look effortless and easy," but this all starts with commitment, because without commitment, nothing ever happens. How do you expect to be great at something and have it reflected in your bank account when you always have one foot in the door and one foot out? Life doesn't work like that for top performers. In every industry, the ones who are committed and who have the strongest work ethic always rise to the top in anything. I know people with the most random jobs who out-earn people with prestigious jobs, you could say, based on a worldview perspective. *I will, I must, I can be* is the attitude you must attain to rise to the top. When you get tired, keep going, because we will all be tired for good one day, and we don't know when that's coming. We all have one life to live, so why not live it to the fullest and make it the absolute best and create what we want to create? Make a difference in someone else's life and touch their heart by what you do. The effort will play a big part in the lives of all of us.

Are you putting effort into things you want to accomplish? That has always been the big thing for me. I can feel the lack of energy right away when I'm not into it. When we look at everything as a whole, like why I am upset right now, and especially how this whole pandemic has changed things and people's perspectives, it's all about division: getting people fired up on each side so they can divide people and turn them against one another. The devil's best thing is to isolate people, make them feel like they're no good, and turn them against one another over a matter of opinion. What were we all doing before all this unfolded? Can you think of a time when you thought things would be closed because of certain rules, especially here in Canada? That shouldn't deter you from doing something great in your life right here and now. You still have a lot to give as long as you breathe. Personally, when I have been down and not felt well, it's related to who I have been surrounding myself with to a certain extent. Your surroundings play into your thoughts and frame of mind big time. By hanging around a bunch of miserable people, sooner or later that will rub off and you too will start to feel miserable. Jim Rohn said it best when he said you're the total of the five people you most hang out with. This concept relates to an animal-type instinct of wanting to fit in with the pack and be part of the gang. People will sacrifice for what they truly believe in and bite their tongue to remain in the pack, even though they might disagree, because everyone wants to fit in to a certain extent.

As I have gotten older, I have made it a point to speak the truth, and if people don't like it, then so be it. I can't please everyone. Sometimes people ask me, "Why are you so aggressive?" I'm a man with testosterone running up and down my body. It's an instinct not to back down and fight for what I believe in. If you look at how young men and women are today compared to fifty years ago, so many things have changed. I truly believe that if you want to start living life to the fullest then form a relationship with God, there will be no greater force when you are down, than having God by your side and knowing what he has in store for you. People have sins. People have flaws. We all do, but with God, there is no mistake; there will be no greater feeling when you feel that energy rush into your heart. This feeling will be like no other. As I always say, "When a man turns a certain age, it's time to leave boy stuff behind." It's amazing how I run into people I have known for ten years, and they're doing the same shit. It's like, "No, bro, I haven't done any of that shit in years. My life over the last so many years has been self-development." How do I become the best version of myself I can be to become the hero of my own story? What are the things I tell myself? How do people view me when they first approach me? People lead by strength. The most you can do is attack every day like it's your last. How do I put myself in a position to win? Let me ask you this: How do you truly expect to win if you don't eat, breathe, and dive depths into the core of what you were created to do? Adapting to a high level will affect your life in every area to an inclination of abundant thoughts and unstoppable results.

Other things can also lead to unhappiness, such as drugs, alcohol, or whatever your vice is. Ask yourself this:

If you are currently doing whatever you frequently do, do you feel good the next day? Do you feel a seed of happiness waking up, or do you feel a seed of depressive thoughts coming in, like *Why did I do that? I feel like shit now; my head is pounding,* or *My stomach feels ready to explode.* Honestly, do you think doing this daily will benefit you long term and give you this everlasting fire of going out to tackle the day? So frequently nowadays you see people lost in space somewhere while they are at work. Ask yourself this, for whatever it may be for you: Do you like yourself when you're sober? Or do you simply put on a mask every day and have something take you to a state of mind, that for a short period, gives you a sense of peace and takes you away from all the things going wrong with your life? Here is the thing: the devil works overtime in everything he does. He will meet us in the parking lot and at the dinner party. There is no time or place he will not stop trying to take control of our thoughts so he can keep us not moving forward, and not pursuing what God intended for our life.

Over time, as I have come to understand, not everyone is a follower. Hey, I don't judge anyone, because if I do, I too shall be judged. Some people believe in the air, in the trees, in a variety of different types of energy, and the list goes on. I like to hear from every category as long as it promotes love at the end of the day. I've never been the type of person to be closed off; I'm always open to hear something from someone else. When you look at any romantic relationship, understand that looks fade. Someday we will all wake up, and we won't be as pretty as we once were. We will have to rely more on a loving personality to get us through the rough days because our partner won't be so pretty anymore from a physical standpoint. When you form any relationship with anyone, ask yourself if you love this person's personality. Could you see yourself spending days on end with them? If you have to ponder that question, you might want to reconsider rather than look at the material things or physical attributes this person might have to offer or the benefits they might have in their package. Learn to separate ego from spirituality, because if you drive the relationship based on ego, what will other people think when you're with that person in a relationship? Eventually, something will fail down the line, and it will not be subtle. It's going to be a blow-up-in-your face thing. When you're in a relationship with that person, consider what you think and how you feel about that person because you're the one in it and living it. I am still looking for the one at this point in my life. I would say the relationships I've been in personally have been more based on lust, how we felt about one another sexually, from relationships and flings to encounters, but they've never formed into anything because there was no substance besides that. You may be asking me, "Do you believe you will meet your love? Or do you believe you have already met her?" Part of me wants to say I haven't met her, but another believes I have already met her. To all the fellas out there, if you base your relationship on sex, it's almost always a recipe for disaster; it never works out in the long run.

I don't claim to be a perfect person because I am not. We all have inconsistencies, flaws, sin, and things that make us who we are. As I have gone through the years, I have made an effort to lay it all out on the table and be bold and speak the truth, because people will judge you and me anyways. Why not go down to the mirror of reality and speak the truth into your life, rather than keeping it bottled up, waiting on a rainy day?

The story I mentioned above plays into this, as does being in the hospital with blood clots, but when I hit rock bottom and went off the deep end, I had so many things come against me all at once from relationships to family. It was like a sea of fire heading in my direction, and when it got to this point, I had never felt so alone in my life. I was contemplating ending my life. I knew a spot where I would drive my truck off because I knew I wasn't coming back; I would be better off dead. At that time, I remember my grandpa Frank in heaven speaking to me and reminding me of all those weekends we spent together, talking about the love of Jesus. If I hadn't had him and Jesus in my life from day one, I'm not sure if I would have made it because there were so many dark days when the pain overtook my life. I wished for it to be over.

It's not like I've ever been that bad of a son. I've never been in trouble with the law, never smoked drugs, never stuck needles in my arm, and never tried stuff most children try out. I have smoked the odd cigarette, ripped the cigars, drank tequila and whiskey from time to time, and done some dumb things with weight-loss drugs. Over time though, I have learned to forgive people who hurt me because it has helped me move forward. I can't remain in that space where the pain takes over. It never did me any good, nor would it allow me to heal. I have decided to accept people for how they are; I have prayed that someday they will come around, but at the same time, I'm not going to waste any more time trying to fix it. They have to want to do it for themselves. The man I strive to be like is my grandpa Frank Enright; he was one of the kindest people you would ever meet but he also stood up for what he believed in. What made him so special was that he knew God, and he knew that any problem could be solved with the proper steps if both individuals were willing to work it out. He also knew some completely unacceptable things, and he knew when to move on. I don't buy that old story someone may be telling you, "Oh, I can't change." I'm like, "That's the biggest bunch of bullshit I've ever heard." If people want to change, they will find a way to make a change, but they have to do it for themselves, not anyone else.

So, what led up to all these negative thoughts? I believe that these negative thoughts were a result of all the verbal abuse I encountered over the years from various people. The thing about verbal abuse is that it stays with you because words are power. This will happen if someone tells you over the years that "You will never amount to anything. You're not as articulate as other people. How dare you try to do something like that? If it doesn't work out, you know you will have to do something else." It's like, "No, go piss off and fly a kite."

I'm going to get done what God has planned for my life. People will come out of the woodwork when you have a dream or walk into the unknown. I have had many people shit on me over the years, and the sad reality is it's usually not even strangers; it's the people who are the closest to me. Do something great and see who claps for you; you will have your answer after that.

I had blood clots in the same leg on previous occasions; this big one wasn't coincidental. I was visiting my blood doctor at a university-run hospital. I showed up and met with her, and she decided she wanted to take me off the blood thinners. I said, "Fantastic," because the blood thinner I was taking was warfarin, and the side effects were wild. I was lost on cloud nine most days. But after six months off the blood thinners, I ended up in the hospital fighting for my life in the ICU for close to a month. When I left the hospital, I remember the next four months were a nightmare. Everything I did was like running a marathon. I was slurring my words heavily from having the stroke. It took about a year to feel somewhat normal again, and when I returned to the hospital to visit my blood doctor after this unfolded, the first thing she said to me was, "What happened?" I was like, "What do you mean what happened? You took me off the blood thinners, and this happened." I had never seen such fear on someone's face drop in the matter of a second. I was like, "Don't worry; I forgive you as Jesus has forgiven me." After that, it was almost like she was gasping for air. A sigh of relief rushed into her heart. Guess what, she is way more educated than me, but this time she knew she had made a mistake. But I forgave her so I could move on with my life. We can break the chains of bitterness, hate, and resentment when we forgive.

To this day, what makes me happy is personal development, knowing Jesus, helping people, being a significant person, going fast like Ricky Bobby, and various physical activities. I've taken courses, read books, and studied this stuff for a very long time now. From motivational, spiritual, to religious, and from TV, movies, music videos, to commercials, I've been like a sponge in how the human mind works and in knowing if someone is in character or is breaking character and is full of crap. I am the type of person who will go out of their way for someone. I am a very passionate person. I am well aware of everything around me. I have seen people do one dumb thing after another, but it gets to the point where they have to start helping themselves, not you always being there for them. There is usually meaning and purpose behind everything I do, but when we can positively touch someone's life, that's where it hits home for me. It brings me a great sense of joy when something I was able to do could give another person some hope and joy in their own life. But like anything in life, life is hard. It will be an up-and-down roller coaster. I wish I could tell you if you read this book, you will have this everlasting fire in you. Life isn't constantly a thrill; it will require daily action and work on yourself to get to where you want to go in anything you're doing. But with that said, have a positive attitude throughout the process and love people unconditionally when they do something to hurt you. Understanding what they're doing and not taking it personally will separate you from the "kind of" attitude to the "I must do this no matter what" attitude. I pity people still going on about things that happened ten years ago; why do that to yourself? Why relive that pain for yourself? At the end of the day, it's only hurting you, not them. And you may be saying, "How do I get the ball rolling?" Ask yourself this first: "How is my prayer life?" Prayer plays a significant role in people's self-reflection and in knowing how to fix the problem and move forward. When you can pray, I guarantee you that it will plant a seed inside of you to go out and live an unstoppable life rather than worrying about what could happen. Being told the word "No" really helped me realize this at a young age. You will get knocked down a lot through life.

When I was twelve years old, I started acting in TV, commercials, movies, and music video's I did it until I was twenty-five years old, going to audition after audition and failing time after time. The first commercial I ever landed was a football commercial. The premise was that I was in a school spelling bee and had to spell the word "facsimile." Then, after I spelled it correctly, a famous football quarterback at the time ran and dumped a cooler of water meant to look like an energy drink over my head. This was one of the most incredible experiences of my life. I met him and his family and got an autographed jersey at the end of the day. He was a great and super-friendly guy. I remember I was also doing a photoshoot for a magazine that day, and it wasn't going that great. The football player came in and yelled, "Smile, Man," and immediately after that, everything in that photoshoot started going according to plan.

As the years went by, I did many things from TV, movies, commercials, to music, etc. I never landed any significant role. As I kept going through the process, the weirder it got, and I started to realize how many messed up things were being shown to me through various situations and people; it got to the point where I was getting sick and tired of all the fake things I saw going on, and it made me realize it's not the way I want to live.

Hey, it might not happen for everyone, but it's what I experienced. What I enjoyed about acting, though, was the creativity, taking a character and making it believable for the audience, and also the level of memory I developed by reading scripts and having to memorize so many lines and situations throughout the scenes. I also learned how to be comfortable speaking in front of a lot of people, and I learned how to spot someone's bullshit from a mile away. You may be wondering why I stopped. I guess you could say I was burned out playing different roles and playing different characters. That old saying about the definition of insanity is doing the same thing and expecting a different result. Well, I was sick and tired of being sick and tired. I was sick and tired of people looking from the outside in, saying, "Oh, the acting must be lucrative." Yah, when you're getting parts, but when you're not, it's an uphill battle.

I have had many experiences that made me happy and unhappy, but I have never experienced any greater thing in my life than coming to God. His love for us and joy will create a seed of happiness in every area of our lives. He will help us understand how to look at life from a different perspective. It's a love that's hard to describe to someone else, because it is so personal. When we realize that God loves us unconditionally through all our mistakes, flaws, and inconsistencies, being able to live the life that he intended for us will hit close to home. This will happen when we can finally find that thing we were created to do. When you are really into something, ask yourself how much you know about that topic. I am probably willing to bet that you are like a book of knowledge about that subject, but let me ask you this: Why haven't you been pursuing it? Why haven't you taken that leap of faith and decided to believe that you always had the right stuff and that nothing is impossible with God on your side? Everything is there for you to discover. What would it mean if you could live your best life right now? What would it mean if you could have this unstoppable mindset where anything is possible for your life with the right work ethic and God? How would that make you feel? I would bet, that it would light this fire of greatness you have always wanted to discover. Understand this about the devil, because the devil lies in the details: For most people, the devil lies at your doorstep. He will show up in your thoughts and on your way to work. He will show up in your home. Every negative thing has been a reflection of the devil trying to keep us contained so we cannot move forward. If he can do that, he will have anyone's life right where he wants it. Also, when we look at society, it's not cool to be positive. How often have you watched the news and felt like you were ready to go out and tackle the world after? Does it rarely happen? Life is like a garden: it will let you reap what you sow. It's like going out tomorrow and saying, "Well, it's going to be a shit day. It's cold out." Fuck this kind of attitude. How well do you think your day will go after all that negative talk? Whether we plant a seed of positivity or a source of negativity, we will get back whatever we plant. You might have planted a seed of something negative, then the more you talk about it, the bigger it becomes; this little mulberry bush might be a full-blown redwood tree now in your mind by the thoughts and things you have been telling yourself about this particular subject or person. The devil loves to keep us all like that. Smack him back and say, "Not today or any day."

But also surround yourself with positive, happy, kind, funny people. I don't have any time to hang out with negative, toxic people. It wastes my time and energy and limits me from moving forward on the things God has planned for my life. Love conquers all; what we choose to focus on will tell us a lot about ourselves and allow us to manifest into our minds by what we choose to focus on. There is no perfect person in this world. We are all flawed; that's why the negative usually outweighs the positive in most cases. The thing I look at is this: How do I react to it? Am I going to let everything go wrong with the world right now affect me? Or am I going to stand and fight no matter what? Understand that this will require daily work and action on yourself if you want to get to that place of positivity in your life. There is a level of importance in significant living and being that once-in-a-lifetime person for other people. Success is great, and you can do many things with it, but it won't help you be fulfilled because success is all about us. However, being a significant person is about other people. When I got my new car, I went and did the deal by myself and took the keys by myself. It was great for a short period. Sure, I was excited at the moment, but eventually, all that thrill that I initially felt when I first got it wore off. The moral of the story is that if you are searching for happiness through material things, though I hate to break it to you, it will be a never-ending cycle. About a year later, a new model will come out that shows more prestige than your car, so then subconsciously you think, "Mine doesn't carry as much value as this new model." What we have to understand when it comes to material things, things that society claims will make us a better person, is that it's all ego driven. You will say, "Oh, if I do this, then what will this person think of me? If I get this big house, what will I look like as a status symbol to other people?" Others will be looking from the outside, going "Oh, wow! Their life must be remarkable by what they have been able to attain in a material aspect." And suppose you hang out with certain people. Others may think, "If this person hangs out with them, they must be important. If this person does this, they must be highly valued, or their significant other is physically attractive. Their life must be all figured out in the sex department." For me, in regard to a romantic relationship, I look at a person's depth. I like to peel back all the layers of someone who wants to get to know themselves deeply. I like going to the hard conversations so we can get to know each other at the core. I am a very passionate person, and many people would call me aggressive, and some frown on that. I'm here once, one time only, so why not make an effort to get to the core root of things and get to the truth at the end of the day? Why fear? It's like seeing someone get mad at someone for something they did that doesn't involve them, but quickly judging them because of disagreeing with what was done or said. Understand that if you judge, you shall be considered for judgment. Before you think about why someone did what they did, ask yourself: "I wonder what this meant for this person, what this meant for themselves, and why they did that?" Because at the end of the day, we don't know what's going on in someone's life unless they decide to open up to us about what's happening.

I'm a very blunt person. I tell it like it is because I understand that as long as I keep doing this, the more I will keep growing as a person and discovering stuff about myself. But there is also a way of saying it so that you don't come off like a jerk; it's not what you say but how you say it. We live in a texting world where most people would rather text someone to try to find a solution. Meanwhile, that never works at the end of the day. The only thing that will do justice is if you have a good old-fashioned conversation with that person, because nothing beats seeing someone in person rather than through a phone or a video call per say. You can express your affection, especially when it comes to love in general and in any relationship, but there is nothing like saying it and showing it in person. People will feel your energy at the end of the day and see that you genuinely care. You can be that once-in-a-lifetime person for someone else. When I wake up every day, I choose to be a significant person. How can I impact someone in a positive way to help them get past barriers and beliefs they might have for themselves? To me, there is no more incredible feeling than doing something for someone else and giving them a sense of happiness in their own life. You will know that you brought some joy to their life; you gave some hope and some peace. They just needed the right person to come along to remind them of how special a person they are rather than feeling down and out about themselves. Strive to be a once-in-a-lifetime person, and you are one of one. When people look at you, one in a million is great, but being able to be that one person who can genuinely help someone with what they are going through like no one else can, at the end of the day, is going to be a pretty special feeling. Know that what you do can impact someone in such an everlasting, unstoppable way. Others can get to the place of happiness within themselves by something that you were able to touch them with along the way.

Understand that through your walk, people need to see that you care. Over time, people will start to look at how you have invested in the relationship, and how committed you are to show up when the time comes, because in today's society, we need more people to care and have a loving personality where you can express your love through different situations. This can be any relationship. Let that person know that you care, you want to help, you want to grow, and you want to have the same love being shown in your life just as much as you show love for them. Love will conquer everything at the end of the day. For every negative thing you come up against, there will always be some form of love waiting to take over for the current pain. You are amazing. Like God always says, "I will always give you somebody." Understand that there is no love like God's love. The amount of love he gives us even when we do wrong, even when we don't understand, is an unconditional love that surpasses any love we will experience here on Earth. We all have flaws, we all have sinned, we aren't perfect. Just when we think something is going all smooth, there will be something right there to get us frustrated and upset. We need to realize how we react to these situations so that they don't consume us and take over our life. Ask yourself how many thoughts come into your mind every single day. I guarantee you that the negative thoughts will try to take over your mind if you let them. What if you could wake up every day and live in a positive state of mind where the happiness keeps pouring into your heart so that the love in your life can take over for good? How would that make you feel at the end of the day? Understand that these exposures will get into our thoughts. What are you allowing to come into this great mind of yours every day? Ask yourself: "Are these things I'm allowing into my mind going to benefit my life in any way, shape, or form?" What if you could wake up and listen, read, or watch something positive when you first rise? What do you think it would do for your health and development over time if you could program your brain when you first wake up to let all these positive thoughts flow abundantly into your life? How do you think, over time, this would affect your life? I guarantee it would plant a seed of positivity in your life, but the choice is yours. Is this something for you? The moral of the story is to do what makes you happy with your life. Nothing will compare when you genuinely start expressing that gift you were given at birth from God. Expressing your gift is crucial to begin living your true self and discovering who you are.

I know people who have the most random job you could think of, and they are successful because they love what they do. They are connected to what they do, and they usually reap the rewards that come with being successful. When you love something, you are willing to go above and beyond what's necessary. You have a fire to push the limits, and it almost becomes game overtime or a chess match, you could say, to make strategic moves and get to the next level. I laugh when people get jealous of other people for being good at something. Maybe this person has recognized their gift. Maybe they are living in their talent. If you are worried about what someone else is doing, you're going to waste a lot of time pondering and questioning what you are great at. We all have something we were born to do, whether someone tells us or not. The mission is too critical to not start expressing what you are genuinely great at, because what you are genuinely great at can help someone for the greater good and touch them in a positive way. You have to be willing to take a jump. I'm not telling you to run out and quit your job tomorrow. What I am telling you, though, is to start doing what you love part-time until it becomes a full-time thing. Even if you don't receive a short-term reward, long-term wins are always worth it in the big picture. Nothing worth having comes easily. Like the old saying, easy come, easy go, but you need to be able to discover that thing that is running deep down in your bones, that thing you are obsessed about at the end of the day. When you talk about it, you get fired up about it in a positive way. We need more people living in their gift and being happy. Progressing a little bit each day will ultimately lead to happiness. For example, think about what you truly love. What is the emotion you feel when you think about this particular thing? How much energy do you have after the fact compared to when you started? When we love doing something, it will give us power and ultimately feed a desire to keep going.

Be passionate. Be committed, stick with the process, and understand there will be ups and downs no matter what. Never give up on your dream at any point. Don't think about how crazy it sounds to other people, because when we look for approval, we look to God. After all, there will be nothing that can compare when you seek support from God and allow him to show up in your life.

For more information, and for speaking services, visit my website: www.awakenthephoenix.global. We strive to help people get past anything they are going through in their life to get to their definition of happiness. Check out my Instagram page, awakenthephoenix_global, for videos and writeups that can be valuable tools for your life to help you become that significant person in someone else's life and the universe. Also, be a once-in-a-lifetime person for others. When others see the clouds in their life, be that person to show them the sunlight. Let them know that you love them simply for who they are. My message to you is to go out there and be a significant, unstoppable, everlasting, gifted, faithful, forgiving, kind, relentless, bold, and truth-seeking believer, evolver, and striver. Be a hungry, one-of-one loving person so that we can not only see the gift that you can share with us but also how many lives you will be able to touch along the way. This is Brett Andrew Miller. Have a great day.